The BIG BUS and US

Alberta Torres

Collins

NEWS &
GAZI

A
BUS
STOP
ES
GROCER

A
BUS STOP

529
B1G 8U5

BUS ROUTES

REPAIRS
BARGAIN STORE
529
B1G 8
AMBULANCE
AMBULANCE

DRY CLEANERS
OPEN
Ballet School
Florist

529
B1G8US

BUS
STOP

BUS GARAGE
Not In Service
B1G 8U5

4
6

DAD
me
MUM
BUS
CAR